MIGHTY MAC

The Bridge That Michigan Built

Jacquie Sewell

Copyright © 2018 Jacquie Sewell

www.jacquiesewell.com

All rights reserved.

ISBN: 978-0-692-98953-1

No part of this book may be reproduced or transmitted in any form without written permission of the publisher.

Michigan Department of Transportation (and Mackinac Bridge Authority) photos used with permission to reprint.
All photos ©State of Michigan (MDOT, MBA) unless otherwise noted.

Poems by David Steinmann used with permission from next of kin to reprint.
"Lake Bottom" and "Types of Bridges" illustrations by Christian Francone.
"Straits of Mackinac" illustration by Catalin Vicol.
"Rolling Wave" photo by Martin D. McReynolds.

Peninsulam Publishing
Publishing stories Made in Michigan

www.peninsulampublishing.com

Printed in the USA

DEDICATION

This book is dedicated with thanksgiving to Jesus, the bridge to eternal life.

I would like to thank my husband, Greg Sewell, whose love and support mean the world to me, and Natalie Iverson, who asked for a book about the Mackinac Bridge and started me on this remarkable journey.

This is the bridge that Michigan built.

"Impossible," the naysayers cried.

"A bridge across the Straits? It could never be built!"

"It's too dangerous!"

"Too far!"

"Too expensive!"

For more than seventy years their objections swirled in the wind and tossed on the waves. The dream of connecting Michigan's two peninsulas languished . . .

... until a group of people had the courage and vision to make the dream come true.

This is the story of the bridge that couldn't be built . . .

but was.

This is the story of the people who overcame every obstacle that man and nature threw in their path and built one of the greatest bridges in the world.

This is the story of the mighty Mackinac Bridge.

This is the man, daring and wise, who said, "Yes, we can!"

and believed in the bridge that Michigan built.

They called him "Mr. Bridge," but his real name was Prentiss M. Brown. He grew up in the Upper Peninsula of Michigan and knew from personal experience that Michigan needed a bridge across the Straits of Mackinac. In the winter of 1920 Brown was a young lawyer working in St. Ignace. He had to cross the Straits to get to Lansing to argue a case in the State Supreme Court. But the ferries were stuck in the ice and the horse and cutter he hired couldn't navigate the 10-foot-high ice-walls jutting up from the frozen surface. Brown and a fellow lawyer set off on foot. They hiked four miles through the wind and snow only to arrive too late to catch their train to Lansing. Brown later said, "That bitter hike across the Straits made a lasting impression on me – for the need of a bridge across the Straits."

Because he believed so strongly in the bridge, Brown was glad to serve as legal counsel for the first Bridge authority in 1934. In 1950 he was appointed the chairman of a newly formed Mackinac Bridge Authority. Their purpose: to find out once and for all if a bridge could be built across the Straits of Mackinac. Prentiss Brown believed the answer was: "Yes!" He worked tirelessly convincing legislators, securing funding, and finding the best engineers, to prove it to the rest of the world.

✦ Prentiss Brown was born and raised in St. Ignace, Michigan.

✦ He was a lawyer, a United States Representative and a United States Senator.

✦ Some people thought Michigan should build a floating tunnel between the Upper and Lower Peninsulas instead of a bridge or "leap-frog" bridges from Cheboygan to Bois Blanc Island to Round Island to Mackinac Island, and finally to St. Ignace.

✦ Before the Mackinac Bridge could be started, the Bridge Authority had to raise almost $100,000,000 (100 million dollars). This huge challenge had to be met by the state's deadline of December 17, 1950. The members of the authority, under Mr. Brown's leadership, secured the financing just in time.

This is the engineer, tried and true, who designed the plan to give to the man who said, "Yes, we can!" and believed in the bridge that Michigan built.

David Steinman is considered by many to be the greatest bridge builder the United States ever produced. Growing up in New York City, he would point to the Brooklyn Bridge, and tell his friends that one day, he too would build a great bridge. And he did. During his lifetime Steinman engineered more than 400 bridges on five continents.

Steinman was one of three engineers hired by the Mackinac Bridge Authority to investigate the feasibility of a bridge across the straits of Mackinac. He measured the force of the wind and the depths of the Straits. He tested rock samples from the lakebed. He ran his calculations and determined a bridge could be built between Michigan's two peninsulas. In 1953, Steinman began drawing up the blueprints for the longest suspension bridge in the world (at that time), the mighty Mackinac Bridge of Michigan.

David Steinman, during the construction of the Mackinac Bridge.

✦ David Steinman was a true "Renaissance Man." He had 14 academic degrees, and was a gifted engineer, mathematician, poet, educator, author, and public speaker.

✦ Six of Steinman's bridges received awards for being among the most beautiful bridges in America.

These are the straits, deep and wide, that were bridged by the engineer who designed the plan to give to the man who said, "Yes, we can!" and believed in the bridge that Michigan built.

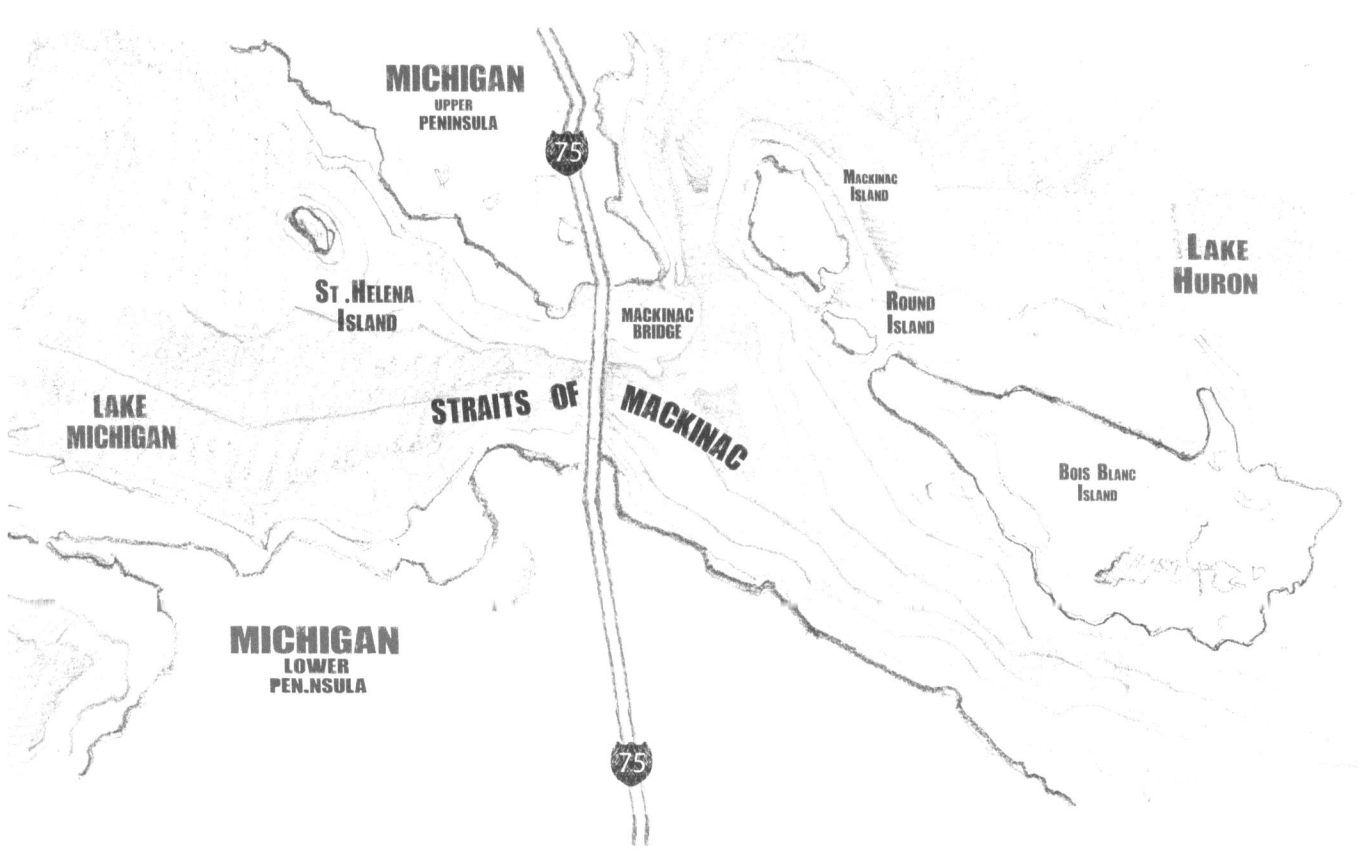

The Straits of Mackinac are four miles wide between Mackinaw City and St. Ignace. Before the bridge was built, ferries traveling between these two cities carried trains and cars across the Straits. They transported people and valuable resources, like copper and iron ore. Great ice crushing ships, the *St. Ignace,* the *Sainte Marie,* and the *Chief Wawatam,* were built so trade could continue even during Michigan's icy winters.

In January 1952, two years before ground would be broken for the bridge, the *Vacationland* arrived in St. Ignace. She was the last ferry built for the state ferry system. Her final day of operation was November 1, 1957, opening day of the Mackinac Bridge.

The Sainte Marie was an ice-crushing ferry that could stand up to the toughest of Michigan winters.

✦ The ice crushing ferries had propellers at both ends and a spoon-shaped bow to ride up and over the ice.

✦ The Michigan state ferry service across the straits was the first ferry service to be operated by a state highway department.

✦ During busy times, like hunting season, the line of cars waiting for a ferry often stretched more than seven miles.

✦ The state ferries operated for 34 years. In that time they carried more than 12 million vehicles and 30 million passengers.

These are the waves, tempest-tossed furies, that fill the straits that were bridged by the engineer who designed the plan to give to the man who said, "Yes, we can!" and believed in the bridge that Michigan built.

(Photo by Martin D. McReynolds)

Storm Facts:

✦ A 750 ton span of roadwork, balancing like a teeter-totter in the St. Ignace harbor, survived the November 16 storm.

✦ Two welding machines and a large pump were ripped from their moorings during the storm and sent to the bottom. Divers later recovered them.

✦ A second storm on December 4, 1955 sank the tug *Lewis,* and wrecked a scow owned by American Bridge.

✦ Because of storms and winter weather, construction on the bridge was usually suspended from mid-December until the ice melted in the spring.

✦ The first year, crews worked at the site until January 14, 1955 to sink the last of the caissons. Within minutes of shutting down for winter, the worst blizzard of the season swept into the straits.

The waters of Lake Huron and Lake Michigan meet in the Straits creating strong currents and unpredictable seas. Storms spring up quickly, often without warning.

Work on the bridge was often delayed for weeks at a time because of weather. On November 16, 1955, construction workers postponed work knowing a big "blow" was coming. But they never expected the hurricane-force winds that ripped through the area that night. Mountains of water pounded the piers attempting to wash away everything in their path. The storm capsized boats, toppled the weather tower, uprooted trees, and destroyed homes. Through the long, dark night the construction crew wondered if the piers and the towers they had labored on for more than two years would still be standing in the morning.

As dawn broke and the storm abated, a cheer went up that could be heard throughout Michigan. The bridge had passed the test! The massive concrete piers and aerodynamic towers of the mighty Mackinac Bridge still stood!

This is the lake bottom, dark and deep and covered with silt, that hides 'neath the waves that fill the straits that were bridged by the engineer who designed the plan to give to the man who said, "Yes, we can!" and believed in the bridge that Michigan built.

The main supports for a bridge have to rest on bedrock, the solid rock foundation beneath most of the earth's surface. Getting to bedrock isn't easy, especially in the Straits of Mackinac.

Not only is the bedrock under 100 feet of water in the Straits, it is covered by the lake bottom, a dense layer of silt, clay, and gravel. In some places this layer, called hardpan, is 105 feet thick.

Two glacial valleys running through the center of the Straits presented another problem for Mighty Mac's builders. Each valley is nearly 3,500 feet wide. In the deepest part of the valleys bedrock is 350 feet below the water's surface.

Reaching bedrock would prove to be one of the greatest challenges for the builders of the Mackinac Bridge.

- ✦ Bedrock is the layer of solid rock that lies beneath the lake's bottom.
- ✦ Workers often used dynamite to loosen the hardpan. Then they could remove it and finally reach bedrock.
- ✦ Huge clamshell buckets operated by derricks scooped up the loosened silt and rock from the bottom of the lake.
- ✦ To visualize the immensity of the glacial valleys, picture 100 school busses in a line. That's how many it would take to go across each valley. It would take 10 school busses to reach from the water's surface to bedrock.

These are the piers, secure and strong, that rise up from the lake bottom that hides 'neath the waves that fill the straits that were bridged by the engineer who designed the plan to give to the man who said, "Yes, we can!" and believed in the bridge that Michigan built.

Clamshell buckets dig out the sand and silt on the lake bottom from inside the dredging well.

Workers in St. Ignace build the frame for one of the cofferdams used to support the towers.

Building piers underwater requires special techniques. For Mighty Mac, cofferdams were used to construct 30 of the piers. They were lowered to the lake bottom in sections and bolted together underwater. Then they were anchored to the bedrock using huge steel spikes (spud piles). The framework was wrapped in steel, creating a watertight chamber. Any debris and hardpan inside the cofferdam was removed with a pipe vacuum. Tons of aggregate (a mixture of sand and gravel) were poured into the cofferdam, displacing all the water inside. Then grout was poured in. As it flowed into and around the aggregate, it forced out the last traces of water. With the help of a "secret ingredient," the grout hardened to create a concrete foundation pier.

In the deepest sections of the Straits, caissons were used to build three of the piers. Picture a huge tin can with a smaller tin can inside. The bottom edges of the two "tin cans" were bent together, creating a closed outer ring and an open inner ring. The inner ring was the dredging well. The caissons were sunk by pouring aggregate into the closed outer ring. The weight of the aggregate pulled the caisson down to the lake-bed. The sharp edges at the bottom of the outer ring cut through the hardpan and into the bedrock like a cookie cutter through cookie dough. Workers used dynamite and jets of water to break up the hardpan and ease the way for the caisson. Once the bottom section was firmly embedded in bedrock, the upper sections were added. The dredging well was then filled with aggregate and grout in the same way as the cofferdams to create a solid concrete pier.

The tops of the bridge piers are eight feet below the surface, safely out of reach of winter's icy grasp. Rising up from the piers are the narrower concrete support pedestals upon which the bridge rests.

✦ Piers 19 and 20, beneath the cable towers, are two of the deepest piers ever sunk in suspension bridge building. They reach down more than 200 feet to bedrock and measure 116 feet in diameter.

✦ Displacement happens when one thing pushes another thing out of its place. The aggregate that was poured into the cofferdams pushed out, or displaced, the water that was inside.

✦ The opening at the bottom of the caisson allows water to rise up inside the center of the caisson. This water pushes against the caisson walls and balances the "push" of the water outside the caisson. If there were no water inside the caisson the force of the water outside would crush it like a paper cup.

✦ The grout used on Mighty Mac was a mixture of cement, sand, water, and flyash.

✦ Caisson 18 was a huge rectangle. It measured 44 feet by 92 feet, and had 21 circular dredging wells, each measuring 9 feet in diameter.

These are the towers, straight and tall, that rest on the piers that rise up from the lake bottom that hides 'neath the waves that fill the straits that were bridged by the engineer who designed the plan to give to the man who said, "Yes, we can!" and believed in the bridge that Michigan built.

Mighty Mac's twin towers rise 552 feet into the air.

Twin towers glinting in the sun, soaring gracefully toward the heavens, rise 552 feet above the water. They are the part of the bridge that everyone notices and remembers.

People admiring the beauty of Mighty Mac's towers may not realize they are also incredibly strong. Strong enough to support 38,486 tons. That's the weight of the roadway plus the huge cables that hold it up and the estimated weight of the vehicles traveling across the bridge at one time.

Due to their height, the towers were built in sections and assembled on site. A special crane, called the Creeper, was used to lift each section of the tower into place.

✦ Service elevators in each tower allow maintenance workers access to the top of the towers.

✦ The towers are crowned by 34-ton "saddles." The saddles support the cables that hold up the roadway.

✦ The steel in the towers expands with the summer's heat. Expansion joints allow the towers to "grow taller" without damage.

These are the cables, spun like yarn, that stretch down from the towers that rest on the piers that rise up from the lake bottom that hides 'neath the waves that fill the straits that were bridged by the engineer who designed the plan to give to the man who said, "Yes, we can!" and believed in the bridge that Michigan built.

Workers measure the diameter of one of the cables high atop the Straits.

✦ Laying of the cables began July 18, 1956 and finished on October 19, 1956.

✦ Seven hundred reels of wire were used in the Mackinac Bridge. Each reel weighed 16 tons and held 330,000 feet of wire.

✦ Each cable contains 37 bundled strands. Each strand contains 340 wires clamped together.

✦ Mighty Mac is a combination of suspension bridge and truss bridge construction.

42,000 miles of wire make up Mighty Mac's support cables. That's enough wire to wrap around the earth twice. Laying the cables was called "spinning" because of the two large "spinning wheels" that shuttled back and forth between the North and South anchor piers carrying the wire. As a safety precaution, cowbells were attached to the spinning wheels. Their clinking sound warned the men to duck or step aside to avoid getting hit in the head.

Wire ropes, suspended from the finished cables, hold up the roadway.

At five miles long, Mighty Mac is one of the longest suspension bridges in the world.

This is the roadway, of concrete and steel, that's supported by the cables that stretch down from the towers that rest on the piers that rise up from the lake bottom that hides 'neath the waves that fill the straits that were bridged by the engineer who designed the plan to give to the man who said, "Yes, we can!" and believed in the bridge that Michigan built.

The two inner lanes of Mighty Mac's roadway and the dividing strip between them are an open steel grid. This design was part of Steinman's strategy to make Mighty Mac strong enough to weather any storm. The open grid allows the wind to blow freely above, below, and through the bridge, making it virtually invisible to the wind. Even winds greater than 600 mph won't topple Mighty Mac.

✦ The last section of the roadway was lifted into place on May 17, 1957 at 3:55 p.m.

✦ The total roadway is 54 feet wide. The vehicle lanes are 46 feet wide.

✦ Walkways on each side of the roadway are for bridge personnel only.

✦ Hikers, bikers and snowmobilers must be transported across the bridge in Bridge Authority vehicles.

These are the machines, carried by boats, that built the roadway that's supported by the cables that stretch down from the towers that rest on the piers that rise up from the lake bottom that hides 'neath the waves that fill the straits that were bridged by the engineer who designed the plan to give to the man who said, "Yes, we can!" and believed in the bridge that Michigan built.

Gismo, seen here, was invented just for the Mackinac Bridge construction job.

Building Mighty Mac posed many challenges because of the deep waters of the straits. To meet those challenges unique machines and techniques were developed by the engineers and workers.

Gismo :   Building piers in the glacial gorge that runs through the middle of the Straits called for some creative engineering. Two young engineers invented an unconventional way to drive in the bearing piles (steel support beams) that held the cofferdams and caissons in place. They called it the Gismo.

Gismo was a triangular shaped contraption that supported the bearing-pile at the correct angle while a huge 10-ton steam hammer pounded the pile into the bedrock. Gismo could drive a 125 foot pile through 100 feet of hardpan into bedrock in just 30 minutes, a job that normally took four hours by the old method. Blasts of compressed air moved the water out of the way so the full force of the hammer blows went into the pile. The noise created by these blows could be heard at the surface through 70 feet of water. Fish were stunned and even killed by the force. They soon learned to avoid the waters around the bridge.

The Creeper lifting a section of the tower.

The Creeper: There were two Creepers on the site, one at each tower. Awkward looking contraptions, they were instrumental in erecting the towers of the Mackinac Bridge.

Each Creeper had two diesel lifting-engines mounted on a platform at the bottom of the bridge tower. These lifting-engines hoisted the "creeping" assembly up the tower shaft where it was bolted to the tower. At the very top was a 90 foot boom and a huge block-and-tackle which acted like a crane to lift the next section of the tower into place. As the tower grew higher and higher, the Creeper kept "creeping" upward until it lifted the last section into place.

The Creeper was capable of lifting 100 tons of steel 80 feet above itself. Because of the extreme weight being lifted, the Creeper was only operated in calm weather. High winds or rough water could have turned the Creeper into a 100 ton wrecking machine.

Algonquin and *Prepakt Jr.*: Once a cofferdam or caisson had been secured to bedrock and its inner wells filled with aggregate, it was ready for *Algonquin* or her sister ship, *Prepakt Jr.* These floating mixing-plants carried the equipment that mixed and delivered the grout used in Mighty Mac's piers. Together these two ships supplied all the grout needed to produce all the concrete in Mighty Mac - more than 900,000 tons.

✦ The Prepact method of making concrete calls for placing the aggregate first and adding the grout separately. This method was used on the Mackinac Bridge piers. It saved time and money and resulted in a much harder and denser concrete than conventional methods.

These are the men, hard-working and brave, who operated the machines, that built the roadway that's supported by the cables that stretch down from the towers that rest on the piers that rise up from the lake bottom that hides 'neath the waves that fill the straits that were bridged by the engineer who designed the plan to give to the man who said, "Yes, we can!" and believed in the bridge that Michigan built.

Shift change at the bridge construction site.

The Surveyors: Before any construction could begin at the straits, surveyors had to mark the exact locations for each pier and tower. First they built fourteen surveying towers, eight on land and six in the water. From the tops of these towers they could measure and "triangulate" the positions for the bridge supports. This very complicated process took two full seasons of work by the survey crew. Apart from storms, the biggest threat to the surveyors was the seagulls nesting on Green Island where one of the survey towers stood. These territorial birds resented the intrusion into their privacy and the survey crew became daily "targets" of the flock's displeasure.

The Merritt-Chapman and Scott Co. Foundation Crew: Few people will ever see the work of these men. Most of it is hidden beneath the waves. Under the direction of Grover C. Denny, the foundation crew corralled caissons, sank cofferdams, tightened almost a million bolts and poured 451,000 cubic yards of concrete. When they were finished, only a row of concrete pedestals rising out of the water, gave evidence that they had been there.

The Divers

More than half of Mighty Mac is under water. The engineers and crew members depended on divers to be their eyes and hands in places they could not reach.

When the cement began leaking out of one of the caissons, it was a diver who discovered the buckled plate and went below to fix it.

When storms hurled valuable equipment to the bottom, it was a diver who retrieved it.

When a caisson got stuck in the hardpan, it was a diver who planted the dynamite to loosen it.

When a bolt needed tightening, it was a diver who went down with the wrench.

And when a steel rod needed shortening, it was a diver who held the torch.

Getting a diver into his waterproof suit and helmet (not shown) required a little help from his friends.

Without the divers, the Mackinac Bridge couldn't have been built.

Walking across trusses, high above the Straits, was part of the job for this steel worker.

The American Bridge Co. Steel Workers: Steel workers came from all over America to work on Mighty Mac. Some were just out of high school, others were seasoned professionals. Balanced precariously 500 feet in the air, they set beams, welded trusses, "spun" cables, and topped the towers of the mighty Mackinac Bridge.

A bronze statue of an ironworker was unveiled at Bridgeview Park during the Bridge's 50th anniversary. Scores of ironworkers returned to St. Ignace to celebrate and be celebrated. Many of them echoed the words of Bob Britton who said, "I really feel privileged and honored to have been part of building the Mackinac Bridge. It was something that many people said couldn't be done, but we did it. It was one of the finest jobs I have had."

Off-Site Workers: More than 2,500 men worked at the bridge site, but three times that number worked off the site. They dug up the stones and sand needed for the concrete, milled the steel, and built the massive caissons and cofferdams that became the piers. In all, more than 10,000 people helped build Mighty Mac.

"A Bridge Demands a Life"

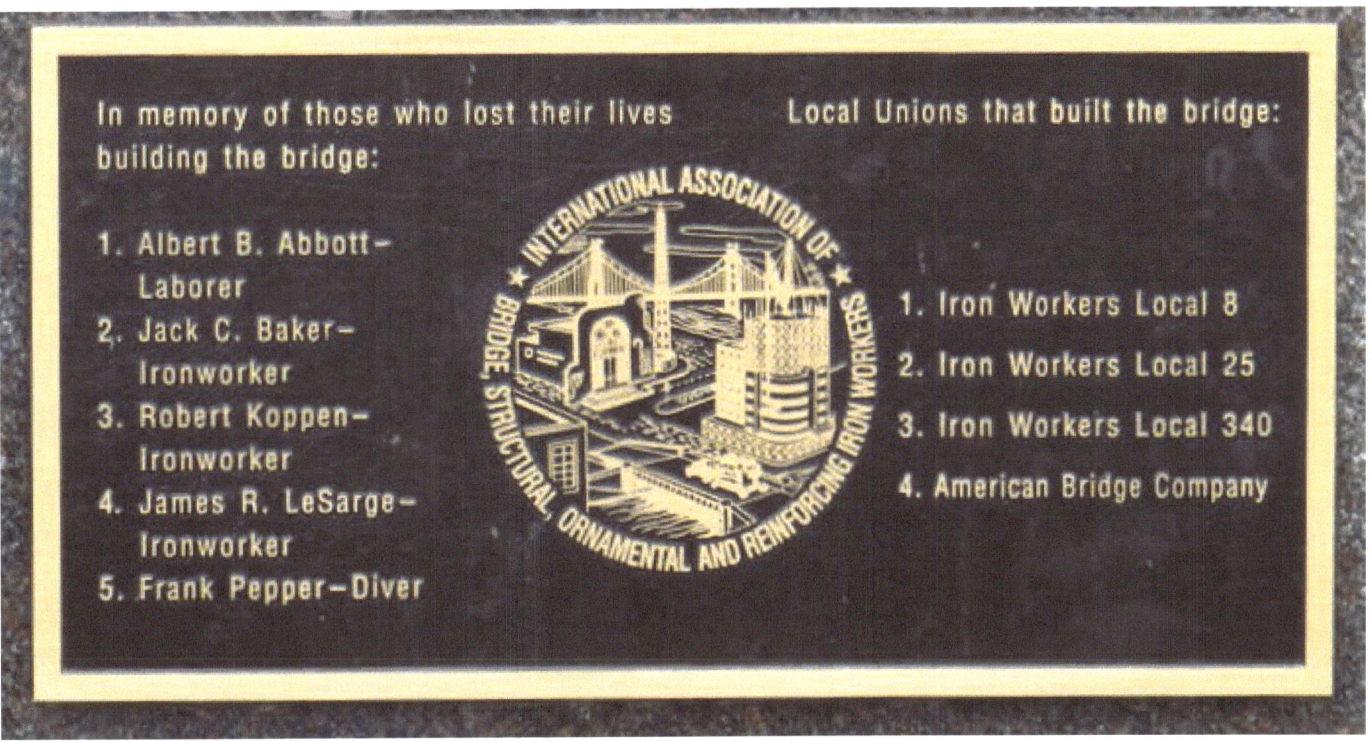

The five men who died during the construction of the bridge are remembered with a bronze plaque at each of the bridge approaches.

Bridge building is a dangerous occupation. In spite of modern safety precautions, contractors estimate that one life will be lost for every million dollars of construction. For the Mackinac Bridge, that would have equaled almost 100 deaths. Thanks to the vigilance and care of the engineers and workers, that prediction was thwarted.

Five men died in the construction of the Mackinac Bridge. Contrary to popular myth, no one is buried in the foundation of the bridge.

Frank Pepper, a diver, died of the bends after inspecting the foundation depths on September 16, 1954.

James R. LaSarge, a welder, died after falling into a caisson on October 10, 1954.

Albert B. Abbott, a laborer, drowned in one of the pier cofferdams on October 25, 1954.

Jack C. Baker, an ironworker, fell from a catwalk at the North Tower on June 6, 1956.

Robert Koppen, an ironworker, fell from a catwalk at the North Tower on June 6, 1956.

These are the people: families and tourists, hunters and fishermen, businessmen and laborers, who owe a debt of thanks to the men who operated the machines, that built the roadway that's supported by the cables that stretch down from the towers that rest on the piers that rise up from the lake bottom that hides 'neath the waves that fill the straits that were bridged by the engineer who designed the plan to give to the man who said, "Yes, we can!" and believed in the bridge that Michigan built.

People are allowed to walk across the bridge on just one day every year - Labor Day. The Labor Day Bridge Walk started in 1959. Every year since, the Governor of Michigan has led participants in the 5 mile walk from St. Ignace to Mackinaw City.

On average, 40,000 to 65,000 people take part in the Labor Day bridge walk. A record-setting 85,000 people turned out for the walk in 1992, when then-President George H.W. Bush also participated.

When walkers complete their journey and reach Mackinaw City, they receive a "Certificate of Completion."

The 1951 Chevrolet Station Wagon that Al Carter drove across Mighty Mac on November 1, 1957, is on display at the Grand Rapids Museum. (Photo by Greg Sewell)

On November 1, 1957 Michigan's two peninsulas were finally united when the Mackinac Bridge officially opened to traffic. Michigan's "miracle bridge" was a success. The first person, after Governor Williams, to drive across the bridge was Al Carter, a jazz musician from Chicago. Carter's lifelong hobby was being first at everything.

Every year almost 4 million vehicles travel across the straits, safe and secure, 199 feet above the water on the mighty Mackinac Bridge.

✦ During their last year of operation ferries carried 900,000 vehicles across the Straits of Mackinac. During 1958, its first full year of operation, Mighty Mac "carried" more than 1,390,000 vehicles across the Straits.

✦ The 100 millionth vehicle crossed the bridge on June 25, 1998.

✦ July and August are the busiest months with an average of 567,389 vehicles per month crossing the bridge.

✦ January and February are the slowest months with an average of 174,880 vehicles per month crossing the bridge.

✦ 3,914,361 vehicles crossed the Mackinac Bridge in 2015.

This ironworker, sculpted by Janice Trimpe in honor of all the bridgemen who worked on Mighty Mac, stands in Bridge View Park in St. Ignace, Michigan.

TYPES OF BRIDGES

There are seven types of bridges used around the world. Each type has different strengths and purposes. Some bridges, like the Mackinac Bridge, combine two or more types of construction. Mighty Mac use both truss bridge and suspension bridge construction.

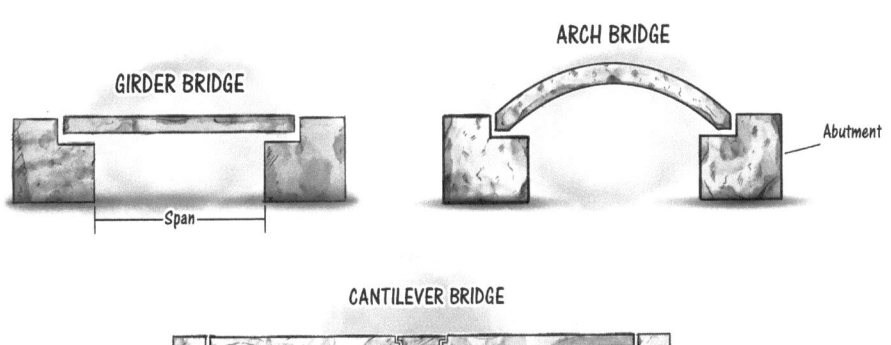

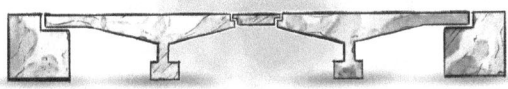

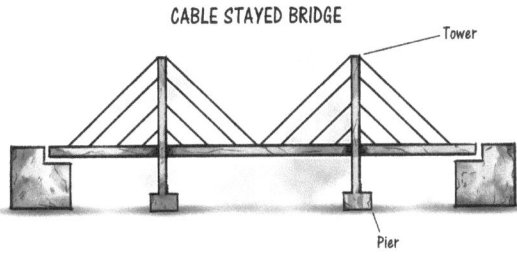

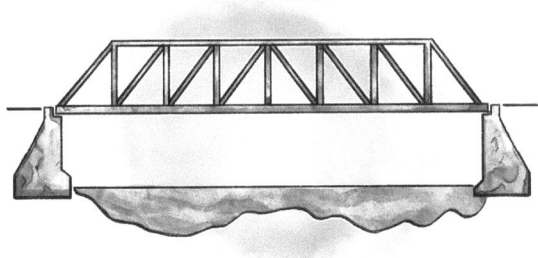

Girder Bridge: These are the simplest bridges to build. They are also the oldest type of bridge. Girder bridges are basically a deck (roadway) supported by girders (steel or iron beams). A log across a creek is a very simple girder bridge. The log is the deck and the banks of the creek are the girders.

Arch Bridge: Arch bridges are the second oldest type of bridge and among the most beautiful in the world. As their name suggests, an arch provides the main support for the bridge deck.

Cantilever Bridge: A cantilever is a structure that extends horizontally out into space, supported only at one end like a balcony. Cantilever bridges have a section in the middle that appears to be unsupported. The primary supports for this type of bridge are at the shore ends.

Cable Stayed Bridge: A cable stayed bridge is a type of suspension bridge. In a cable stayed bridge the cables that support the deck attach directly to one or more towers.

Suspension Bridge: Suspension bridges are the best choice for spanning great distances. Vertical cables suspended from strong cables that run between high towers support the weight of the deck in a suspension bridge. The Mackinac Bridge uses both truss bridge and suspension bridge construction.

Truss Bridge: In a truss bridge the deck is supported by a framework of steel beams. The trusses can be above or below the decking.

The Bridge at Mackinac
By
David B. Steinman

In the land of Hiawatha
Where the white man gazed with awe
At a paradise divided
By the straits of Mackinac -

Men are dredging, drilling, blasting,
Battling tides around the clock,
Through the depths of icy water,
Driving caissons down to rock.

Fleets of freighters bring their cargoes
From the forges and the kilns;
Stone and steel - ten thousand barge-loads -
From the quarries, mines and mills.

New the towers, mounting skyward,
Reach the heights of airy space.
Hear the rivet-hammers ringing,
Joining steel in strength and grace.

High above the swirling currents,
Parabolic strands are strung;
From the cables, packed with power,
Wonder-spans of steel are hung.

Generations dreamed the crossing;
Doubters shook their heads in scorn.
Brave men vowed that they would build it -
From their faith a bridge was born.

There it spans the miles of water,
Speeding millions on their way -
Bridge of vision, hope and courage,
Portal to a brighter day.

Poems beginning each chapter of Dr. Steinman's book *Miracle Bridge at Mackinac*

I built a bridge across a gulf
To hail my fellow man;
I found in him a kindred spark -
He helped me build the span.

Generations dreamed the crossing;
Doubters shook their heads in scorn,
Brave men vowed that they would build it -
From their faith a bridge was born.

Nature said: "You cannot."
Man replied: "I can."
From shore to shore above the tides,
He built a gleaming span.

When man first flung a log astride a stream,
He leapt millenniums beyond his birth;
Now strands of steel translate his lofty dreams
To link the farthest corners of the earth.

Help me, Lord, to build my span
Across the chasm of the years;
Firm in purpose, true in plan,
Above the drag of doubt and fears.

Man built a bridge -
From caissons deep below the swirling tides,
Majestic pylons interlaced with light
Rise proudly upward to the azure vault
To hold a harp outstretched against the sky,
A poet's dream against the sunset gold -
To reach the stars.

Anchored firm in solid rock,
On Thy foundation let me build -
Strong to bear each strain and shock,
An arch of dreams and faith fulfilled.

Help me build on Thy high road
A bridge to serve the common good,
To smooth the way and lift the load,
A link of human brotherhood.

With hammer-clang on steel and rock
I sing the song of men who build.
With strength defying storm and shock
I sing a hymn of dreams fulfilled.

In human heart was born the plan;
A bridge of peace, uniting man.
Our sons will have the span we wrought;
The world the dream for which we fought

A bridge of strength and grace in mystic blend
Embodies spirit treasures that transcend
The steel and stone; the builder's dream is there,
Each curve a song, each soaring line a prayer.

I lift my span, I fling it wide,
And stand where wind and wave contend,
I bear the load so men may ride
Whither they will, and to what end.

Now the towers, mounting skyward
Reach the heights of airy space.
Hear the rivet hammers ringing,
Joining steel in strength and grace.

Between the towers reaching high
A cradle for the stars is swung;
And from this soaring cable curve
A latticework of steel is hung.

I built a bridge across the tide
To gain the farther shore,
And there I came on fairer glens
Than any glimpsed before.

Against the city's gleaming spires
Above the ships that ply the stream,
A bridge of haunting beauty stands -
Fulfillment of an artist's dream.

Around the bridge is an afterglow
The city's lights like fireflies gleam,
And eyes look up to see the span -
A poem stretched across the stream!

Mine and quarry yield their treasures;
With sweat and blood, with hope and prayer,
We forge the steel and hew the stone,
And conquer wind, and bridge the air,
We do not waver.

We labor not for instant pleasure;
Our sons will bless our toil and sorrow.
For them this span when we are gone
A pathway to a bright tomorrow.
We build forever.

The light gleams on my strands and bars
In glory when the sun goes down.
I spread a net to hold the stars
And wear the sunset as my crown.

GLOSSARY

Aerodynamic: Having a design that reduces the forces of the wind moving past.

Aggregate: Crushed rock used to form bridge piers.

Bearing Piles: A strong support column, usually of steel, concrete, or wood, driven into the ground to support the weight of the structure.

Bedrock: Solid rock underlying loose surface deposits of soil, silt, etc.

Caisson: A watertight structure, built offsite, and floated to the construction site, inside of which construction work can be carried out under water; caissons are better suited than cofferdams for deep water construction.

Catwalk: A narrow, temporary walkway that allows workers to access elevated areas.

Cofferdam: A watertight enclosure, built onsite, that allows underwater construction work to be done inside it.

Derricks: A crane with a movable arm used to lift heavy objects.

Dredging well: Open, inner ring of a caisson which allows hardpan to be removed from inside the caisson and which is later filled with aggregate and grout to create a pier.

Glacial Valley: A steep U-shaped valley formed by the erosive forces of a glacier (a large, slow-moving mass of ice).

Grout: A mortar of cement, sand, and flyash used to bind aggregate together.

Hardpan: A hardened layer of soil, usually rich in clay, at or below the surface.

Peninsula: A piece of land surrounded on three sides by water.

Renaissance Man: A person who has wide-ranging interests, and is an expert in several fields of knowledge.

Spud Piles: Steel beams used to anchor caissons and cofferdams to bedrock.

Straits of Mackinac: A narrow waterway connecting Lake Huron and Lake Michigan that separates the two peninsulas of Michigan.

The bends: Also called "caisson disease;" a painful and often fatal condition caused by nitrogen bubbles in the blood, a result of a rapid decrease in atmospheric pressure, as when ascending too quickly from a dive.

Triangulate: A surveying technique using the geometry of triangles to establish the distance between, or relative position of, two points.

ABOUT THE AUTHOR

www.jacquiesewell.com

Jacquie Sewell was born in Green Bay, Wisconsin, so it is inevitable that she loves all things cheese, and green and gold.

She is married to Greg Sewell and is blessed to be the mother of Josiah and Micah Sewell.

The gift of reading came to her early - even before kindergarten she was reading the cereal box and anything else she came across. She still can't pass a bulletin board without stopping to read all the posts! The gift of writing followed soon after.

Even before she could write she would dictate stories to her mother. She finds the world around us to be a beautiful and inspiring place filled with amazing creatures and
brave and courageous people.
Sharing their stories with children is her passion.

She is a children's librarian, now retired. It was in the school library where Jacquie was asked the question that led to *Mighty Mac: The Bridge That Michigan Built.*

Be sure to check out these other educational, Michigan-focused children's books from

Peninsulam Publishing

www.peninsulampublishing.com

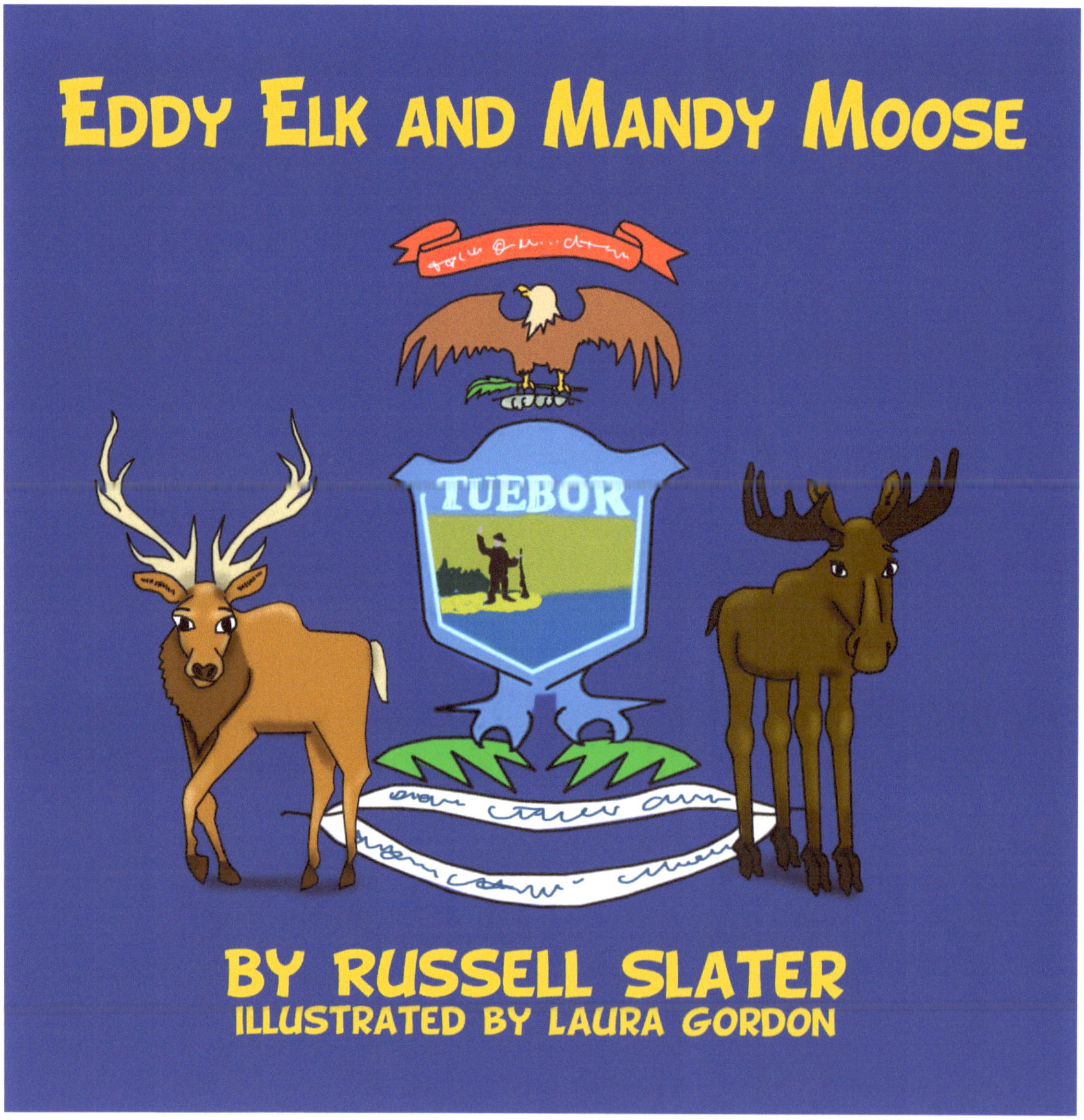

EDDY ELK AND MANDY MOOSE

BY RUSSELL SLATER
ILLUSTRATED BY LAURA GORDON

Eddy Elk and Mandy Moose have stepped out of the flag, they're on the loose!

Join the adventurous pair as they explore the natural wonders of the Great Lakes State. From the Petoskey stone to the Whitetail deer, learn why there is no place on Earth quite like Michigan.

U.S. $9.99

What's so "great" about the Great Lakes State? EVERYTHING!!!
From lake to glistening lake, this precious pair of peninsulas holds a special place in the hearts of those lucky enough to call Michigan "home."

Join us on a journey across the state and learn why we're proud to say,

"I'M A MICHIGANDER!"

U.S. $12.99

"What's that blue flag?

Why, that's our Michigan flag, and it's full of meaning!

Step into my classroom and let me tell you all about it…"

U.S. $9.99

Take a peek at the pleasant peninsula treasured by Michiganders both north and south of the Mackinac Bridge.

From the Pictured Rocks, to the Soo Locks...

The U.P. awaits you and me.

Michigan's Upper Peninsula: It's like a whole other state!

U.S. $9.99

www.ingramcontent.com/pod-product-compliance
Lightning Source LLC
Chambersburg PA
CBHW041411160426
42811CB00106B/1674